Anonymous

Constitution and By-Laws of the Celtic Society of Montreal

Anonymous

Constitution and By-Laws of the Celtic Society of Montreal

ISBN/EAN: 9783337296865

Printed in Europe, USA, Canada, Australia, Japan

Cover: Foto ©Suzi / pixelio.de

More available books at **www.hansebooks.com**

CONSTITUTION AND BY-LAWS

OF

INAUGURAL ADDRESS OF THE PRESIDENT,

LIST OF MEMBERS, Etc.

Organized Dec. 6th, 1883.

Montreal:

W. DRYSDALE & CO., PUBLISHERS.

1885.

OFFICE-BEARERS.

Honorary President:

REV. PRINCIPAL MACVICAR, D.D., LL.D.

President:

REV. DR. MacNISH, CORNWALL.

Vice-Presidents:

J. LEWIS, ESQ., AND J. K. WARD, ESQ.

Recording Secretary:

C. McKERCHAR.

Corresponding Secretary:

WM. GREIG, SR.

Treasurer:

REV. W. J. DEY, M.A.

Executive Committee:

REV. PROF. COUSSIRAT, B.D., B.A.	J. W. McKENZIE, B.A.
D. McTAGGART, ESQ.	MR. D. McLEAN.
A. MacLENNAN, ESQ.	WM. DRYSDALE, ESQ.

Bard:

MR. ARCHIBALD McKILLOP.

CONSTITUTION.

I.

This Society shall be known as the CELTIC SOCIETY OF MONTREAL.

II.

The object of the Society shall be the promotion of the study of the Celtic Languages and Literature.

III.

Its members shall be confined to the following classes :

(*a.*) Gentlemen and Ladies who by authorship, public addresses, or otherwise, have given evidence of their interest or eminence in Celtic studies.

(*b.*) Corresponding, Honorary, and Life-Members.

IV.

The office-bearers of the Society shall be an Honorary President, a President, two Vice-Presidents, Recording Secretary, Corresponding Secretary, and Treasurer, to be elected by ballot at the annual meeting; said office-bearers, along with six members annually chosen in the same manner, shall form an Executive Committee for the transaction of business between the regular meetings of the Society.

A Bard shall also be appointed at the first meeting, to hold office during the pleasure of the Society.

V.

The President shall occupy the Chair at meetings of the Society, be *ex-officio* a member of all Committees, and discharge such other duties as belong to his office. In his absence one of the Vice-Presidents shall take his place.

VI.

It shall be the duty of the Recording Secretary to keep the minutes of all meetings of the Society, and to do such other clerical work as may be laid on him from time to time. The minutes to be kept in English.

The Corresponding Secretary shall conduct the Correspondence of the Society.

VII.

The Society shall hold an annual meeting, the time and general character of which shall be determined by resolution.

VIII.

By-Laws may be adopted or amended at any regular meeting of the Society, notice having been given of such amendment at a previous meeting.

IX.

This Constitution may be amended at any annual meeting of the Society by two-thirds vote of members present, provided that notice be given of the amendment in the circular calling the meeting.

BY-LAWS.

I.

Members shall be admitted by ballot at any meeting of the Society—a majority of the votes present to constitute a member.

II.

The annual fee for ordinary membership shall be one dollar; and the revenue from fees, after defraying the current expenses of the Society, shall be expended in the purchase of Celtic books to be placed in the College library for the use of members.

III.

One payment of twenty-five dollars to the funds of the Society shall entitle to Life-Membership.

IV.

The regular meetings of the Society shall be held monthly, from October to March inclusive, for hearing papers, readings, recitations, debates, &c., upon subjects fitted to promote the interests of the Society.

V.

Special meetings may be called at any time by the Executive Committee.

VI.

The Society may, from time to time, offer such prizes for competitive essays, examinations, &c., as shall be agreed upon at any regular meeting.

VII.

The ordinary rules of debate shall be followed in the conduct of all meetings of the Society.

VIII.

The Society shall, if deemed advisable, from time to time publish its Transactions.

INAUGURAL ADDRESS

BY

REV. DR. MacNISH,

President Celtic Society of Montreal.

GENTLEMEN :

I beg to return my best thanks to you for the honour which you have conferred upon me in appointing me President of this Society. My regret, however, is great and sincere, that you did not select some one to fill the honourable office which I now hold, who has a wider and more thorough knowledge of the Celtic languages than I can pretend to have, and who has more leisure for attending to the various requirements of a youthful Society like ours ; inasmuch as, even with large zeal and enthusiasm on the part of members of our Society, constant vigilance and earnest diligence are needed to impart permanent strength and usefulness to our Society. We have a large and an intelligent constituency, however ; and, such being the case, we can in all fairness hope, that our Society, which is still in its infancy, will go on to gather strength, until it reaches the years, and gathers the usefulness, of a courageous and vigorous manhood.

Those whose hearts are warmed with Celtic blood have at least the satisfaction of knowing, that they are the descendants of perhaps the oldest race in Europe. Although the earliest appearance of the Celts on that Continent is enveloped in hopeless obscurity, it is true beyond contradiction that our Celtic forefathers were both numerous and powerful, and had the hoar and honour of centuries on their side, before the English or German or French or Italian peoples had any distinctive existence. Pride of extraction and veneration for genealogies that reach back into the distant past, seem to possess a strong and a strange fascination for the human heart. In the social life of modern days, there is a tacit admission, that any one is entitled to more than ordinary respect, who can prove that the blood of many illustrious generations is coursing in his veins. In his very instructive lecture on the *Peopling of Europe* (p. 7), Professor Campbell remarks, with reference to the extravagant claims to a very remote origin which are made by the Welsh and Scotch and Irish : "We smile at these pretensions to antiquity, and treat them with the incredulity that most of them deserve ; but we have little to put in their place beyond vague conjecture. That Celts, Germans and Sclaves came originally from the East is a truth requiring little more ingenuity to discover than that the dawn springs in the same quarter into day. But how they were known in the East, and how they travelled westward, and when they reached their present seats or their historic homes : these are questions that are still almost unanswered." With a larger measure of truthfulness and applicability, perhaps, than he had in contemplation, these well-known words of Horace are predicable of the Celts :

> Vixere fortes ante Agamemnona
> Multi : sed, omnes illacrimabiles
> Urgentur ignotique longa
>   Nocte, carent quia vate sacro.
> Paulum sepultæ distat inertiæ
> Celata virtus.

Many magnanimous and heroic Celts there doubtless were in the unrecorded past,—Celts whose names and prowess are buried in the grave of stern oblivion, because no memorial of them was committed either to stone or verse,—Celts who, so far as subsequent generations are concerned, and so far as the efforts of Celtic scholars to penetrate the far-off past are concerned, exemplify with painful accuracy the saying of Horace, that "virtue or valour, when it is uncelebrated, is removed but a short distance from buried listlessness." Max Müller thus tersely and lucidly describes the history and the present position of the Celts : " The Celts seem to have been the first of the Aryans to arrive in Europe ; but the pressure of subsequent migrations, particularly of Teutonic tribes, has driven them towards the westernmost parts, and latterly from Ireland across the Atlantic. At present the only remaining dialects are the Kymric and Gadhelic. The Kymric comprises the Welsh and Cornish, lately extinct, and the Armorican of Britanny. The Gadhelic comprises the Irish, the Gaelic of the west coast of Scotland, and the dialect of the Isle of Man. Although these Celtic dialects are still spoken, the Celts themselves can no longer be considered an independent nation like the Germans or Sclaves. In former times, however, they not only enjoyed political autonomy, but asserted it successfully against Germans and Romans. Gaul, Belgium and Britain were Celtic dominions, and the north of Italy was chiefly inhabited by them. In the time of Herodotus, we find Celts in Spain ; and Switzerland, the Tyrol, and the country south of the Danube, have been once the seats of Celtic tribes. But after repeated inroads into the regions of civilization, familiarizing Latin and Greek writers with the names of their kings, they disappear from the coast of Europe. Brennus is supposed to mean king, the Welsh *brennin*. A Brennus conquered Rome, B.C. (390), and another Brennus threatened Delphi, B.C. (280). And about the same time a Celtic colony settled in Asia and founded Galatia, where the language spoken at the time of St. Jerome was still that of the Gauls."* The earliest settlers of any permanence in a country are wont to leave behind them indelible reminiscences, in the names of mountains, lakes and rivers. It is to the careful dissection of the Celtic languages that the philologist must needs have recourse, to determine where those languages were at one time spoken ; over what area they extended, and what relations they bear to the classical languages of the ancient world. Topographical names are to be found in Europe and elsewhere, which

* Science of Language ; 1st Series, p. 198.

are manifestly Celtic, and which justify the inference, that the Celts inhabited at some time or other those places where such names still exist, having been carried over the centuries to our own day. Though much that is fanciful and that cannot bear rigid examination, may enter into the reasoning, and conclusions of enthusiastic Celts respecting the early greatness and prowess of their race, it cannot be doubted, that a very fertile and attractive field is offered to the careful scholar by the topography of the countries with which the Celts may have had an intimate connection. In a work entitled "The History of Celtic Languages,"—a work which is, perhaps, but little known, though its author displays no small acumen and scholarship and ingenuity,—the student can discover a fair example of what a warm enthusiasm can accomplish. The author contends that *e.g. Heber* is probably a compound of *oin* or *ain*, river, and *bar* or *bhar*, beyond. The term *Heber*, therefore, means to cross over, is simply the opposite side, and is the equivalent of *Inver*, a word which is commonly found in the topography of Scotland. The presence of *bo* or *ba*, cow, is with apparent correctness detected by the same author in such words as *Bohemia*, *Boeotia*, *Bavaria*, *Batavia*, *Bashan*, *Bosphorus*. So confident is the author that his argumentation is solid, and that every intelligent reader must accept it, that he thus invites the reader to attend while he is unfolding the manner in which fowls obtained their names: "Let us now, in prosecution of our plan, attend to Adam giving names to fowls." So certain is the author that his explanation of names of fowls on the ground of Onomatopoeia is satisfactory, that he avers : "If it should be denied that we have proved the Adamic origin of the Celtic, it is undeniable that we have proved the natural origin of it, and certainly nature was prior to Adam."

"Lo! the trunk, rearing from its parent earth,
And now to branches numerous giving birth :
Such is the Celtic tongue; an Eden oak,
Supplying nations from its hoary stock."

Sir William Betham, in his interesting work, "The Gael and Cymbri," gives a long list of topographical names in Asia and Europe, which, according to his contention, are Celtic, *e.g.* Tyre, means land or country, *Tir.*
Sidon or Saida is from *Saida,* a seat or site.
Italy is from *ith,* corn, and *talamh,* country: the land of corn.
Dalmatia—*Dal,* share or tribe, and *maith,* good.
Sardinia—*Sard,* the greater, and *inis,* an island.
Corsica—*Corsad,* coast.
Baleares—*Ba,* cows, and *lear,* the sea.
Lusitania—*Luis,* flowers, and *tana,* country.
Astures—*As,* a torrent, and *tir,* a country.
Cantabri—*Ceann,* head, *tiar,* high above, and *bri* a hill.

There can be no question, that the names of many of the rivers of Spain are Celtic ; that such names of mountains as *Alps, Apennines, Pennine, Pyrenees* are Celtic ; and that such French rivers as *Rhine, Rhone, Garonne* and *Seine* are likewise Celtic. Tiber, the classic river of Italy, bears an unmistakable likeness to the Irish *Tipra,* as in Tipperary, and to the Gaelic *Tobar.* Even so learned and painstaking a scholar as Latham contends that the word *Aborigines* is Celtic, and that he discovers in *Abor,* the *Aber* which occurs so frequently in such names as Aberfoyle, Aberdeen, etc. The word Portugal seems to bear its Celtic origin on the very face of it, *Port nan Gaidheal.*

More than half a century has elapsed since Prichard's famous work, " The Eastern origin of the Celtic nations," was published, forming as it did, perhaps, the first serious attempt that had been made to determine, on philological principles, the position which the Celtic languages ought to occupy in the great family of languages. Prichard was successful in vindicating the claims of the Celtic languages to be classed in the same category with the Greek, the Latin and the Sanscrit languages. To the important contribution to Celtic philology, which was thus made by Prichard, material aid was subsequently rendered by Pictet, whose work on " The affinity of Celtic Languages with the Sanscrit" appeared in 1837 ; and by Bopp, whose work on " The Celtic Languages" was published in 1839. To German scholars, too much praise cannot be given for their profound and painstaking investigations in the field of Celtic literature. Among all labourers in the domain of Celtic philology, the first place is, by common consent, assigned to Zeuss, whose marvellous " Grammatica Celtica," the result of unremitting toil and investigation during thirteen years, was published in 1853. Zeuss wrote his grammar in elegant Latin, and displayed an unusual ability in wielding the language of Cicero and Tacitus, even when he had to deal with the minutest particles, and with the relative value of half-forgotten Celtic adverbs and conjunctions. No English translation of the "Grammatica Celtica" has yet appeared. That admirable work of Zeuss, indicating, as it does, a vast comprehension of intellect, a masterly power for examining even minute details, and a patient and laborious research which rose above every obstacle and fatigue,—will henceforth be regarded, in all probability, as the foundation of scientific Celtic philology. Ebel, who prepared a second edition of the " Grammatica Celtica " and published it in 1871, and Windisch, are German scholars to whom Celtic philology is much indebted. In our own day there have appeared many able and industrious Irish, Welsh, Gaelic and Manx scholars, who, stimulated in many cases by the extraordinary diligence and researches of German philologists, have done much, and are doing much, to redeem Celtic literature from the imputation of being insignificant in itself, and of having among those whose inheritance it is, few who care sufficiently for it to study it, and to bring its beauties and its treasures to the light of modern intelligence.

Were a comparison instituted between the condition of Celtic learning in Great Britain and Ireland when Prichard's well-known work was published, or even when Zeuss gave to the world his admirable " Grammatica Celtica," and the manner in which Celtic literature is now cultivated by those whose venerable inheritance it is, it would be found that a vast improvement has taken place in a commendable direction ; and that, *mutatis mutandis*, to Celtic scholars in the study of their own literature, the description which Virgil gives of a sight that Æneas witnessed as, himself unseen, he looked upon those who were rearing the walls of Carthage — the city of Dido, is to a large extent applicable :

> "Instant ardentes Tyrii ; pars ducere muros,
> Molirique arcem, et manibus subvolvere saxa.
> O fortunati ! quorum jam moenia surgunt."

The fondness for claiming a very remote antiquity which pervades the members of the Celtic family, is exemplified in the well-known story of a MacLean, who, when the conversation turned on the deluge and the manner in which its ravages were avoided, maintained, that the MacLeans disdained to take shelter in the Ark, for the very good and independent reason that they had a boat of their own.

In the preface to his " Grammatica Celtica," (p. 11), Zeuss states, " that the Irish language claims for itself the first place and the largest diligence in the cultivation and study of it, not only in consequence of the larger fertility of the forms of the language, but also in consequence of the more abundant monuments that have been preserved in old Irish MSS., by which the British MSS. of the same age, or rather the Welsh (which doubtless are the only MSS. that reach the age of the Irish MSS.), are far excelled as well in number as in the fulness of their contents."   To the explicit authority of Zeuss every deference must be paid.   There is thus a compliance with the Irish proverb, *dean gach aon duine buidheach ma fheudair :* " make every person grateful if it be possible."   Irish legends assign a very early date to the peopling of Ireland by Partholan, Nemedh, Firbolgs, Tuatha de Danann, Gaels, Milesians, or Scots : here are the names of the leaders of immigrants that found their way, at different times, into Ireland, or of the tribes themselves, which, according to the legends of Ireland, arrived at different periods in that country.

There is an Irish saying, *Inmain tainig o thir tenn*— "Beloved is he who came from a brave land," which applies to the far-off ancestors of the Irish people. The ancient literature of Ireland is vast and varied. Irish writers were wont to speak of the *hosts* of the books of Erinn. Though many of those old books have been irreparably lost, there still exists an immense quantity of Irish literature. In the Libraries of Ireland and England, as well as in Continental Libraries, there are numerous Irish MSS. To obtain even an imperfect knowledge of the more useful portions of Irish literature demands a large expenditure of time and pains. Among the many industrious and able and patriotic Irish scholars of this century, there is one in particular whose name is to be mentioned with every respect—one whose memory is to be gratefully cherished by every student of Irish literature,—one who brought to bear on the literature of his country an extraordinary amount of industry and patience as well as ability,—one who has constructed, by his indefatigable exertions, an easy path for all who may desire to have some knowledge of the literary treasures of Ireland— one who was as modest as he was scholarly and patriotic. I refer to the late Eugene O'Curry, the first professor of Irish History and Archæology in the Catholic University of Ireland. Matthew Arnold pays this beautiful tribute to the great and modest Irish scholar : "Obscure Scaliger of a despised literature, he deserves some weightier voice to praise him than the voice of an unlearned belletristic trifler like me : he belongs to the race of the giants in literary research and industry,—a race now almost extinct. Without a literary education, and impeded too, it appears, by much trouble of mind and infirmity of body, he has accomplished such a thorough work of classification and description for the chaotic mass of Irish literature, that the student has now half his labour saved and needs only to use his materials as Eugene O'Curry hands them to him." It was in 1860, that O'Curry's Lectures on the MSS. Materials of ancient Irish History were published. Mr. Skene, one of the ablest Celtic scholars of our day, thus praises O'Curry's Lectures : "They are most interesting and instructive, and for the masterly and complete survey taken of the subject as well as for accurate and minute detail, they are almost unexampled in the annals of literature." The student reads with unmingled admiration for the modesty, the patience and the ability of O'Curry, his Lectures to which I have just referred as well as his Lectures on the Manners and Customs of the Ancient Irish. The latter Lectures he was not allowed to publish, for his career came to a sudden end. Dr. Sullivan, another Irish scholar of reputation, has performed the duties of editor with remarkable faithfulness, and with commendable reverence for the worth of O'Curry. O'Curry was an Irish Gael of whom every Celt has reason to be pardonably proud. In his preface to the Lectures which he himself was able to edit, he says : " When the Catholic University of Ireland was established and its staff of professors, from day to day, announced in the public papers, I felt the deepest anxiety as to who the professor of Irish History should be, if there should be one. * * * At this time, however, I can honestly declare that it never entered my mind that I should, or ought to be, called to fill this important situation, simply because the course of my life in Irish History and Antiquities had always been of a silent kind. No person knows my bitterly felt deficiencies better than myself. And it never occurred to me that I should have been deemed worthy of an honour which, for these reasons, I should not have presumed to seek." Such are the modest terms in which O'Curry speaks of himself; though a casual glance at his Lectures will suffice to convince any intelligent reader that his labours were enormous ; that his ability for deciphering old MSS. was remarkable ; and that, not only his fellow countrymen, but all lovers of Celtic learning, owe him a very deep debt of gratitude indeed. William Livingstone, perhaps the most talented Gaelic bard of this century, thus extols O'Curry :

> " Eirinn uaine tog do cheann,
> 'S na bi' nis mo fo ghlasaibh teann ;
> Do chainnt oirdheirc oil do'd chlainn
> A thogas cliu le gloir neo fhann,
> Air Eoghan gu buaidh.
>
> Tha tir nam beann 's nan tuil an gaol ort,
> Sean Albainn chruaidh na morachd aosda,
> 'Toirt furain duit le lamhan sgaoilte,
> A dh' aineoin co their nach faod i
> Eoghain gu buaidh. "

Leabhar na h-uidhre, The Book of Leinster, The Book of Ballymote, The Leabhar breac, the Yellow Book of Lecan, The Book of Lecan, The Book of Lismore—such are the principal books of ancient date that pertain to Irish literature.

Leabhar na h-uidhre, or the book of the dun (dark grey), is said to have received its name from the fact, that Fergus Mac-Righ, who was an Ulster prince of great fame, appeared after his death and recited the *Tain Bo Cuailgne*, or the cattle prey of Cooley in Louth—a tale which is, by common consent, allowed to form the Iliad of Irish Literature. St. Ciaran, thereupon, wrote down the tale at the dictation of Fergus in a book which he made from the hide of his pet cow. The cow, from its colour, was called the *odhar* or dun cow, and from that circumstance the book was ever afterwards known as *Leabhar na h-uidhre*.

2.—Of the *Book of Leinster*, which was composed in the early part of the 12th century by Finn, Bishop of Kildare, O'Curry writes in warmest terms of praise, maintaining that there was not in Europe any nation save the Irish, that would not long since have made a literary fortune out of such a volume.

3.—*The Book of Ballymote* was written in the County of Sligo, about the close of the 14th century. It is said that there scarcely exists an O' or a Mac at the present day, who may not find in the Book of Ballymote the name of that particular remote ancestor whose name he bears as a surname, as well as the time at which he lived, what he was, and from what more ancient time he again was descended.

4.—*The Leabhar breac*, or Speckled Book, appears to have been written in Duna Doighre, on the Galway side of the Shannon, about the close of the 14th century, by members of the literary family of the MacÆgans.

5.—*Leabhar buidhe Leacain* was compiled about 1390, by a family of MacFirbises, in Sligo.

6.—*Leabhar Leacain* was compiled in 1416, in Sligo, by *Gilla Isa Mor MacFirbis*.

7.—*The Book of Lismore* is so called because it was discovered in 1814, by workmen who were employed by the Duke of Devonshire in repairing his ancient Castle of Lismore, in the County of Waterford.

The Annals of the Four Masters: Such is the name of a monument of Irish learning and patriotism to which there attaches a peculiar interest, owing to the circumstances amid which it was composed and the comprehensive purpose which it seeks to accomplish. O'Curry thus writes : " In whatever point of view we regard these Annals, they must awaken feelings of deep interest and respect, * * * as the largest collection of natural, civil, military and family history ever brought together in this or perhaps any other country." It was John Colgan who gave the name, *The Annals of Four Masters*, to that work which was composed principly by four friars of the order of St. Francis, in the County of Donegal. The Annals of the four Masters, written in Irish Gaelic, begin with the deluge which, following the Septuagint, they date Anno Mundi, 224. The Annals come down to the year 1616, and, therefore, embrace 4500 years of a nation's history. Sir James MacIntosh thus commends the Annals of the Masters : " No other nation possesses any monument of literature in its present spoken language, which goes back within several centuries of these chronicles." The Annals of the Four Masters, the result of most patriotic faithfulness and unremitting diligence, beautifully verify the statement which Michael O'Clery makes in the Dedication : "Nothing is more glorious, more respectable, or more honourable than to bring to light the knowledge of ancient authors." *Nach ffuil ni as glormaire, agus as airmittnighe, onoraighe ina fios seandachta na seanughdar.*

John O'Donovan, another Irish scholar of great learning, has edited *The Annals of the Four Masters* and has added very useful annotations. Todd, Hennesey, Petrie, Joyce, O'Looney : such are the names of other Irish scholars who have done much in various channels of research to advance the cause of Irish learning. There is a legend to the effect that Finn MacCumhaill was, upon a certain occasion hunting near *Sliabh nan Ban*, in the County of Tipperary. As he was standing near a well, a strange woman appeared and filled a silver tankard at the well. Finn followed her unperceived, until she came to the side of a hill, where a concealed door opened suddenly, and she walked in. Finn attempted to follow her, but the door was shut so quickly that he was only able to place his hand on the door-post with his thumb inside. It was with great difficulty that he was able to extract his thumb, which bruised as it was, he put into his mouth to ease the pain. No sooner had he done so, than he found himself possessed of the gift of foreseeing future events. This gift was not always present, but only when he bruised or chewed the thumb between his teeth. Such is the history of the phrase, *Finn's thumb of knowledge,* and of the aphorism :

> " *Tabhair tordog fod' dhead fis*
> *Is na leig sinn an eislis.*"

> "Put thy thumb of knowledge to thy tooth
> And leave us not in ignorance."

When we interpret that aphorism in its practical sense, it is to be cheerfully admitted that the Irish scholars of our day are doing earnest honour to it. Dr. Joyce, among others, has done much in his *Irish Names of Places* to excite the interest of Celtic scholars ; to show how the topographical names of Ireland were formed ; and to verify the motto which he has adopted, " *Triallam timcheall na Fodhla*, Let us travel round Ireland." His lectures leave no room to doubt, that those who gave names to the various places in Ireland spoke pure Gaelic, and were accurate observers of the physical peculiarities of that country. So successful have been the efforts of the Society for the preservation of the Irish language already been, that Irish Gaelic is now taught in the Schools of Ireland, and that patriotic and enlightened members of that Society have gained for Ireland the commendation of Horace: "*Prima feres Ederae victricis praemia.*"

Thomas Stephens, the learned author of the *Literature of the Kymry*, states that Welsh or Walsch is not a proper name, but a Teutonic term signifying *Strangers*. The Welsh or, Kymry,— which he contends is the correct designation, are the last remnant of the *Kimmerioi* of Homer and of the Kymry, the *Cimbri* of Germany. From the Cimbric Chersonesus, (Jutland,) Stephens further avers, a portion of the Kymry landed on the shores of Northumberland ; gave their own name to the County of Cumberland ; and, in the process of time, followed the seaside to their present resting place, where they still call themselves Kymry, and give their country a similar name. Regarding the obscure, though very important question, as to whether the Kymry preceded the Gaels in their occupation of Britain, it is possible to cite the authority of two very able Welshmen in favour of the theory, that the Gaels must have preceded the Kymry. The topographical names of Great Britain and Ireland go to prove that Celts who spoke Gaelic must have occupied those countries for a sufficiently long time to give to the prominent headlands and mountains, and bays and lochs, and rivers, the names that they still bear.

Edward Lhuyd, the famous author of the *Archaeologia Britannica,* who expended five years in travelling among those portions of Great Britain and Ireland where the Celtic languages were spoken ; who is justly regarded as the father of Welsh philology, and whose important services are thus commended by one of his Celtic admirers :

> *" Unde feres tanto molimine grates,*
> *Vel quae sint meritis dona paranda tuis !"*

writes: "Nor was it only North Britain that these Gwydhelians (Gaels) have in the most ancient times inhabited, but also England and Wales: * * * and our ancestors did, from time to time, force them northward. From the *Kintyre* of Scotland where there are but four leagues of sea, and from the County of Galloway and the Isle of Man, they passed over into Ireland, as they have returned backward and forward often since. Whoever takes notice of a great many of the names of the rivers and mountains throughout the Kingdom, will find no reason to doubt that the Irish must have been the inhabitants when those names were imposed."

Professor Rhys, of Oxford, himself a Welshman and a Celtic scholar of large attainments, thus writes (*Celtic Britain,* p. 212, 213,) with reference to inscriptions that are to be found in Wales: "The Celts who spoke the language of the Celtic Epitaphs were *Goidels,* belonging to the first Celtic invasion of Britain, and of whom some passed over into Ireland and made that island also Celtic. * * * Some time later there arrived another Celtic people. These latter invaders called themselves Brittones and seized on the best portions of Britain, driving the Goidelic Celts before them to the west and north of the island. * * * Their Goidelic speech, which was driven out by the ever-incroaching dialect of the Brythones, was practically the same language as that of the Celts of Ireland, of Man, and of Scotland." When Welsh scholars of the acumen and scholarship of Lhuyd and Rhys concede, that the Gaels must have preceded the Kymry in the occupation of Britain; and when the inference is quite natural that those writers always deferred to the spirit of the Welsh proverb : " *My cheri gy fofni gyvyeith*," " Thou wilt not delight to put one of the same language in fear;" it may be maintained, that honest argumentation can lead to no other conclusion than this,—that the evidence which is available points distinctly to an earlier occupation of Britain by Celts who spoke Gaelic. There is no likelihood, however, that scholars who hold a different theory respecting the arrival of the earliest Celts in Great Britain, will be content to acquiesce in the opinions of Lhuyd and Rhys, without making a further effort to substantiate their own views. The Welsh aphorism has manifold applications : *Kudvyt keissyessyt keissyadon*, " As long as there will be things to seek for, there will be seekers." In the preface to his " Grammatica Celtica," Zeuss asserts that "it can by no means be established that there was a fellowship or an identity of language between the British and the Irish (Brittannos *et* Hibernos), in the 8th or 9th century ; nor even at a much older date, although it is abundantly manifest that both dialects or languages have begun from one fountain." The Welsh have a copious literature. As well in prose as in verse, they have many works of venerable antiquity, and, therefore, of great value and interest. To the Kymry, justice is merely done, whenever it is said, that for faithfulness to their language and their traditions; for a resolute determination to uphold their language and to cultivate it assiduously in these modern days ; for a liberal recognition of excellence in writing the Welsh language either in verse or in prose ; for a refreshing absence of everything that betokens a desire to ignore or forget their language ; for a well-arranged system to make every Welshman proud of his language and his people and country —the palm has to be cheerfully awarded to them among the Celts of Great Britain and Ireland. The name of the Rev. Griffith Jones will be ever dear to every patriotic Welshman ; for he was the first who made any successful attempt to erect

Schools for the instruction of the people in their own language. Mr. Jones began his patriotic work in 1730, and devoted himself for thirty years to that work with the gratifying success of establishing 220 Schools during that time. It may, roughly speaking, be said that from the departure of the Romans in 446, A.D., until Llywellyn Ap Gruffydd was killed in 1282, and with him the liberty and independence of Wales were lost; the Welsh had to fight *pro aris et focis*. It is Taliessin who says :

" Ban gwir pan disgleir,
Bannach pan lefeir."

" High is truth when it shines,
Higher when it speaks."

Frequently during the centuries that intervened between the departure of the Romans from Britain, and the overthrow of Welsh independence, the *Brythonic energy arose. Brythonic Yniwis dydyrchefis.* The Welsh muse found congenial and continuous employment in celebrating the victories of the Kymric princes. Thus vast accessions to the poetical literature of Wales were made.

The Welsh *Eisteddfods* or *Eisteddfoddau*, those sittings, or Sessions, or Congresses of bards, or literati, which are now held almost every year, must have an immense power so far as inducing the Welsh people to love their language, and their literature, and the traditions of their country, is concerned : so far as determining to be faithful to their nationality is concerned : so far as refusing on grounds of strict utilitarianism to forget their language, and to ignore or think lightly of their literature, is concerned. " When I see," writes Matthew Arnold, " the enthusiasm these Eisteddfods can awaken in your whole people, and then think of the tastes, the literature, the amusements of our own lower and middle class, I am filled with admiration for you." It is said that the Gorsedd or Assembly from which the Eisteddfod has sprung, is as old as the time of Prydain, the son of Ædd the great, who lived many centuries before the Christian era. Several Eisteddfods were held in the remote past. It is said of Rhys ab Tewdwr who assumed the sovereignty of South Wales in 1077, that he brought from Britanny to Wales the system of the Round Table, and restored it with regard to minstrels and bards as it had been at Caerleon upon Usk under the Emperor Arthur. The Welsh Eisteddfoddau exercise a most healthful influence in stimulating the literary ambition of the more intelligent and thoughtful of the Kymry. Those annual gatherings and the prizes which are offered in connection with them, had much to do in inducing Thomas Stephens, the Eugene O'Curry of Welsh literature, to give to the world the benefit of his extensive knowledge of the literature and traditions of his country. The Prince of Wales offered a prize in 1848, to be given at an Eisteddfod at Abergavenny, for the best Essay on the literature of Wales during the twelfth and succeeding centuries. Stephens was successful in gaining the prize which was thus offered. His Essay, now known as the " Literature of the Kymry," is regarded as one of the most important contributions that has ever been made to Welsh literature. After writing other works on various subjects, Stephens died in 1875.

It is affecting to learn, on the authority of his biographer, that when the Eisteddfod was held at which he gained the prize that the Prince of Wales offered, the bardic name which was attached to the Essay was read out, and the silence of expectation was most painful ; for Archdeacon Williams, of Cardigan, as he rose to make the award, declared " that a new star was to appear that day in the literature of Wales." Again the name rang through the building ; and then a young man, with marks of severe study upon his face, rose and announced that he was Thomas Stephens, the author of the successful Essay.

A large number of Welsh MSS. exists. With the exception of the MSS. that are in the British Museum and in the Libraries of Oxford and Cambridge, the Welsh MSS. that are extant are in private collections. There is the Hengwrt collection, which bears that designation in consequence of its being made by Robert Vaughan, of Hengwrt. Jones, another collector of MSS., and Vaughan agreed, that on the death of one of them, the survivor should become possessor of the whole collection of MSS.

To what is known as the "Myvyrian Archæology of Wales," a very interesting history attaches. Owen Jones, to whose patriotism and indomitable energy the honour belongs of preparing and publishing the "Myvyrian Archæology," was a native of Myvyr. From his childhood he had a remarkable affection for the treasures of his country's literature. He repaired at an early age to London, where he pursued the trade of furrier with such perseverance and success, that he amassed considerable wealth which he generously expended in the transcription of MSS. His Archæology which bears the name of his native valley, and which is acknowledged to be the great repertory of the literature of his nation, was published in 1801, and in 1803.

Mr. Skene published in 1868 the four principal ancient Welsh MSS. with an English translation. The four ancient books of Wales comprise :—

The Black Book of Caermarthen, which was written in the reign of Henry II.

The Book of Aneurin, which was written probably in the end of the 13th century.

The Book of Taliessin, which belongs to the beginning of the 14th century.

The Red Book of Hergest, which was compiled at different times in the 14th and 15th centuries.

Mr. Skene has thus presented, in a very intelligible form, the poems of Aneurin, (who exemplifies the faithfulness of the Welsh proverb : "*Ano glew gochlywir*," " He that is brave, his praise will be heard abroad,") and of Taliessin, the poet of excellent forehead, who among the Welsh bards has acquired the pre-eminence of popular reputation; and who in his poem, The Chair of Taliessin, says of himself, "I animate the bold: I influence the heedless: I wake up the looker on: the enlightener of bold kings." In addition to the poems of Aneurin and Taliessin, Mr. Skene's book contains the poems of Llywrach Hen, who is said to have reached the age of 150 years.

There is a galaxy of Welsh scholars whose labours are very important. So wide and diversified, however, is the field of Welsh literature, as is likewise the case with Irish literature; that, even with all the facilities which are afforded by the labour of Welsh and Irish scholars, the gaining of any thing like an accurate knowledge of the literature of Wales or of Ireland demands, even from the diligent student, a vast expenditure of time and pains. *Hoc opus; hic labor est.*

Scottish Gaelic goes back to a very ancient date.

" 'Si labhair Padric 'n innis Fail nan Righ,
'Sam faidh caomh sin Colum naomh tha'n I,
Na Francigh liobhta, 'lean gach tir a mbeus
O I nan deori, ghabh a mfhoglum freimh."

" 'Twas Gaelic Patrick spoke in Innis-Fail,
And sainted Calum in Iona's Isle;
Rich polished France, where highest taste appears,
Received her learning from that Isle of tears."

St. Columba is the most famous Celt of the 6th century. When regard is had to Iona and Lindisfarne, and their long succession of friars and erudite monks and abbots; it may be inferred that Gaelic must have thus enjoyed a patronage at once lofty and faithful; and, that among scholars so renowned and zealous as Columba and his successors were, Gaelic literature reached a high degree of cultivation. Northmen made their appearance in the 9th century and burned the monastery of Iona. In 1266, Edward I. of England, gave orders to destroy the records of Iona. At a later date, he commanded that such records or histories as had escaped his former search should be burnt or otherwise destroyed. Many Gaelic MSS. must have been lost or destroyed during the lamentable days that passed over the Western Isles of Scotland. The Scottish Gaels have no such monuments in prose as belong to the Irish and the Welsh,—who, more highly favoured than the Isles of Scotland, were able to preserve those books which are now so valuable. Mr. Skene has been successful in collecting a large number of Scottish MSS. which are preserved in the Advocates' Library, Edinburgh. It is to be hoped that Professor Mackinnon who, in his Inaugural address, adverts to the work which has to be done in deciphering those MSS., will be able to bring to light some literary treasures of the Scottish Gael of the far off centuries. The Scottish Gaels, however, have Ossian and the poetry of his age. Competent judges will admit, that the poems of the Bard of Selma occupy the first and most honourable place in the entire range of Celtic poetry ; and that, for purity of thought, for chasteness of sentiment, for richness of diction, and sublimity of imagery,—the language which the Son of Fingal applied to his father, the King of Morven, applies to himself and his poetry ;

> " B'aluinn do smuaintean fein, a threin :
> Seasaidh thu, athair leat fein,
> Co e coimeas Righ Sheallama nam feart."

The Ossianic controversy, which was waged with extraordinary keenness towards the close of the last century, is now largely forgotten. James MacPherson, to whom the great honour belongs of collecting the poems of Ossian, and giving them to the world in an English dress, could have preserved the name and honour of Ossian from many a rude assault and many an unfair suspicion. MacPherson did not *forge* the poems of Ossian. Overwhelming evidence is available to show, that long before MacPherson appeared on the scene, Ossianic poems had been in circulation in the Highlands of Scotland. Let *Cothrom na Feinne*, or the *fair play of the Fingalians*, obtain in dissecting the evidence, which pertains to the poems of Ossian, and it must appear, that they belong to a remote past; and that, however great the services were which James MacPherson rendered in bringing those poems in an English attire before the literary world, the distinct affirmation of the celebrated Dr. Blair is to be accepted : " Of all the men I ever knew, MacPherson was the most unlikely and unfit to continue and carry on such an imposture, as some people in England ascribed to him." It was not without carefully weighing the importance of his language, that one of MacPherson's coadjutors in arranging the poems of the Bard of Selma, thus wrote :—" MacPherson could as well compose the prophecies of Isaiah, or create the Island of Skye, as compose a poem like one of Ossian's."

Irish scholars have chosen to employ very warm and severe language in condemning MacPherson, and in pronouncing his Ossian to be a forgery.

Ireland, as Irish scholars assert, must be acknowledged to be the birthplace of Ossian, and the true home of Ossianic poetry. "But it is vain for the perverse of Alba any longer to maintain the field of imposture. I would not dishonour my native language with quotations from Macpherson's jargon :" Such is a specimen of the opinion which an Irish writer advanced in the Transactions of the Gælic Society of Dublin in 1808. So far as the existence of Ossianic or Fenian poems, as he chooses to designate them, in Irish literature is concerned ; there can be no better authority than Eugene O'Curry, who asserts, that there are nine Ossianic or Fenian poems to be found in Ireland before the 15th century. It is clear, therefore, that it is vain to look to Ireland for the originals of the poems of Ossian. Macpherson was never in Ireland, and never had access to Irish MSS. The Dean of Lismore's book, which was compiled about the year 1512, and which was published by Dr. MacLachlan in 1862,—contains no less than 28 Ossianic poems, extending over 2,500 lines,—thus refuting the famous allegation of

Johnson, and exhibiting most satisfactorily that *it* contains a much larger amount of Ossianic poetry than is to be found in the entire range of Irish literature. Fingal and Temora are the longest poems in MacPherson's translation of Ossian. The scene of both poems is laid in Ireland; and, although that is the case, Fingal and Ossian, and their heroes, preserve their distinctive existence as the King and heroes of Morven in Scotland. They are represented as going from Morven to Ireland; and no sooner have they gained their purpose than they return to Selma. There is evidence to show, that before Macpherson's translation appeared, there was an earlier MS. of the poems of Ossian at Douay in Flanders, which contained the poems of Fingal and Temora. The MS. in question was taken from Strathglass in Scotland to Douay. It is a singular fact that when MacPherson's translation of Ossian first appeared, there was residing in Virginia, a native of Mull,—the Rev. Charles Smith, who, when a portion of the Temora was read to him, remarked that he knew the poem, and afterwards repeated a great part of it from memory, intimating at the same time that he remembered such poems from his earliest years. *Moladh gach duine an t-ath mar gheibh.* Let every Scottish Gael persist in believing on the strongest evidence, that Ossian was a Scottish and not an Irish Celt,—that his poems date from an unknown past,—that neither did Macpherson forge them nor did Ireland give them birth, and that the venerable bard of Selma is richly entitled to warm commendations in consequence of his lofty moral teaching, and of the absence from his poems of every semblance of impurity, as well as owing to the magnanimous spirit that animated his heroes in peace and war :

> " Lean gu dluth ri cliu do shinnsearan,
> 'S na diobair a bhi mar bha iadsan."

The Abbe Cesarotti of the University of Padua, who took particular pains to study Ossian and to bring his many beauties before the literary world, says among other things, "The works of the Celtic Homer, *Ossian,* do exist; doubts may be entertained whether Fingal was his father, but no one will say that he was not the son of Apollo." Matthew Arnold thus writes: "Woody Morven, and echoing Sora, and Selma with its silent halls, we all owe them a debt of gratitude, and when we are unjust enough to forget it, may the Muse forget us." Dr. Clerk, in the Dissertation that is prefixed to his excellent edition of Ossian, utters a sentiment in which all the members of this Society will cheerfully acquiesce: "I hope that the time is not far distant when the Scotch and Irish Gael will rejoice in all old Celtic literary treasures as common family property. Nay, the time should be at hand when every inhabitant of Britain will acknowledge the ancient productions of the Celtic muse as part of the national stock."

Dr. Smith's Sean Dana, MacCallum's Ossian, and Campbell's *Leabhar na Feinne,* contain a large quantity of poetry that belongs to the Ossianic era. Since the Reformation, there has appeared a large number of talented poets and poetesses in the Highlands of Scotland. In Mackenzie's *Sar Obair nam Bard Gaidhealach,* there is a fair representation of the poetry of [the principal bards of the last three centuries,—of Mary McLeod and Ewen MacLachlan, of Alexander MacDonald and Duncan Ban MacIntyre, the talented author of *Coire Cheathaich and Beinn Dorain.* In our day, we have the poetess Mrs. Mary McKellar, who can tune the Gaelic lyre with wonderful sweetness, and whose anapaestic metres are worthy of all praise. We have Neil MacLeod, John Campbell, Evan MacColl, and the bard of our own Society. In his *Clairsach an Doire,* which was published a few months ago, Neil McLeod has a beautiful poem entitled: *Am Faigh a' Ghaidhlig Bas.*

> " Duisg suas, a Ghaidhlig's tog do ghuth,
> Na biodh ort geilt no sgaig :
> Tha ciadan mile dileas duit
> Nach diobair thu 's a' bhlar :

Cho fad 's a shiubhlas uillt le sruth,
'S a bhuaileas tuinn air traigh,
Cha-'n aontaich iad an cainnt no'n cruth,
Gu'n teid do chur gu bas."

"Wake up! O, Gaelic, raise thy voice,
Put doubts and fears away,
Ten thousand stalwart friends are thine
To shield thee in the fray.
While glides with murmur sweet the brook,
While beats on shore the wave ;
They'll not consent by word or look
To lay thee in the grave."

Nor are the labourers in the field of Gaelic prose by any means idle. The hundredth anniversary of the birth of Dr. Norman MacLeod, who has come to be known as *Caraid nan Gaidheal,* and whose Gaelic prose is the best in the language, was celebrated in the city of Glasgow a few weeks ago. His confidence in the perpetuation of Gaelic in Canada was so strong, that in the dedication of *Leabhar nan Cnoc,* which was published in 1834, he thus wrote : " *Na creidibh iadsan a tha'g radh gu bheil a' Ghaelig air leabaidh a bais: tha i co slan, laidir, urail, agus a cuisle co fallain 's a bhi i riamh, agus ged thachradh gum biodh i air a fogradh a h-Albainn am maireach, tha farsuingeachd agus fasgadh a' 'feitheamh oirre taobh thall do'n chuan mhor, far am bheil cheana na miltean d'a muirichinn fein a dh' fhailticheadh agus a dh' altrumaicheadh i le solas."* Scottish Gaelic has many able friends who are expending diligent scholarship in the investigation and cultivation of it : such are Dr. MacLauchlan, Dr. Clerk, Cameron, Masson, Nicholson, Skene, Ross, and many more. To the delight of the versatile and energetic Professor Blackie, a Celtic chair has been established in the University of Edinburgh, and Professor Mackinnon has undertaken the duties of the chair with great courage and devotion.

To such an undue length have my remarks already extended, that I must bring my hasty review of Celtic literature as speedily as possible to a close. I must, however, make a brief allusion to Manx, which is the sister of Irish and Scottish Gaelic, and which is worthy of much attention, if for no other reason than this,—that it has lived over many generations and many vicissitudes of political fortune. Owing to its geographical position, which finds fitting expression in its armorial bearing with the motto *Quocunque jeceris Stabo*, the Isle of Man was very much affected by the continual invasions and depredations that were common before and after the tenth century. Among the many explanations that have been given of the word "Man," the interpretation is worthy of notice which bestows on Manannan Mac Leir the honour of giving its name to the Isle of Man. A Manx Ballad contains this allusion to the power which Manannan was supposed to possess of enveloping the island in mist and thus preventing the foe from approaching it.

Cha-n e leis a chlaidheamh rinn e e riaghail
Cha'n e leis a shaighdean no leis a bhogha;
Ach tra fhaicidh e luingeas triall,
Fholuicheadh e mo cuairt leis ceo.

That our cousins, the Manxmen, were able to preserve the semblance of their distinctive nationality, and to continue faithful amid all their harassing fortunes to the language and traditions of their fathers, beautifully indicates that their love for their Gaelic lineage and Gaelic language must have been deep and strong. That the Manxmen could, and can, speak their own Gaelic after bearing the yoke of their Welsh neighbours for 400 years, and the yoke of the Danes for 153 years, and the yoke of the Norwegians for 200 years; and after owning the sway of England and Scotland for 139 years, before the Isle of Man was given to the Stanleys, with whom it remained for 330 years, when it passed into the possession of the Dukes of Athole, who surrendered every claim to it in 1829,—goes very far to show how strong the life of a language is, and how its vitality can continue to be vigorous even when unfriendly forces of a powerful kind are bent on destroying it.

The Manx resembles the Scottish Gaelic so closely that a Manxman and a Scottish Gael can converse easily together in their respective dialects. To Bishop Bedel the honour belongs of translating the Bible into Irish Gaelic; to the Stewarts, father and son, and to Dr. John Smith, the honour belongs of translating the Holy Scriptures into Scottish Gaelic : to Bishop Morgan his Welsh countrymen are grateful for his excellent version of the Holy Scriptures into Welsh. The names of Bishop Wilson, and especially of Bishop Hildesely, with his coadjutors Dr. Kelly and Mr. Philip Moore, ought to be, as they doubtless are, dear to every patriotic Manxman for the excellent translation which they made of the Holy Scriptures into Manx. Manx is written phonetically. No regard is paid to the etymological history or value of its words. The translators of the Bible openly avowed, that their desire was so to spell their language, as to adopt it in its written form to the manner in which it was spoken, that thus the Holy Scriptures could be easily read and understood by every Manxman. No small ingenuity is required in many cases to discover the exact value of certain words and sounds. Irish Gaelic, Scottish Gaelic, and Welsh have been immensely benefitted, in a literary point of view, by the idiomatic and copious phraseology which occurs in the translations that were made of the Holy Scriptures into those languages. The Manx version of the Bible forms the principal portion of the literature of the Isle of Man. It redounds to the credit of Manxmen that in 1858 a Society was formed for the publication of National Documents in the interests of Chengey ny Mayrey; and that already twenty-eight volumes at least have been published by that Society.

From the very imperfect sketch which has now been given of the Celtic literature of Ireland and Scotland and Wales and the Isle of Man, it will be manifest, I hope, that we—the Celts of to-day—have a rich literary inheritance ; and that we owe it to ourselves,—to the honourable demands of a generous patriotism, and to the affection which we ought to cherish for the

homes and writings and traditions of our venerable Celtic
fathers and mothers in the far off centuries,—to appreciate our
literary treasures very highly; to take an affectionate interest
in them ; and, so far as we may have leisure or opportunity, to
gain an accurate knowledge of them ; for, what true-hearted
Celt can deny, that to the literature of his race these words of
Cicero are applicable in all their force : *Cujus studium qui
vituperat haud sane intelligo quidnam sit quod laudandum
putet?* Nor is the statement of Burns otherwise than appropri-
ate wherever Celts do not care for Celtic literature :

> " She honest woman may think shame,
> That ye're connected wi' her."

The Celts on the Continent of America have earned for
themselves a distinguished place in every avenue of toil and
enterprise ; and have repeatedly risen to the loftiest positions
in the learned professions, in commercial pursuits, and in the
administration of Government. It is not only by their sturdy
and manful application to ten thousand forms of industry, but
also by their cultivation of the Celtic muse, that our Celtic
brethren in our own Dominion verify the words of Horace :
Coelum non animum mutant qui trans mare currunt.

Breathing as we do with perhaps too much frequency in
Canada, a literary atmosphere that is impregnated with utilitarianism, the question may be asked by some persons, " What
practical benefits can result from the labours of our Society ?
Will it not be sufficient for us to avail ourselves of the labours
which Celtic scholars are performing across the Atlantic in the
field of our common literature, and to utter sentimental ejacula-
tions of admiration and affection while we ourselves are
studiously idle ?" Apart from the certainty that we must all
agree with Juvenal who says, *Miserum est aliorum incumbere
famae*, it becomes us to act as the Manx saying admonishes us,
Shass er dty chione hene, " rely on your own understanding,"
and to draw together more strongly and sincerely the bonds of

c

literary consanguinity which unite the Celts of Canada. If we are successful in deserving and obtaining the co-operation of the Celtic scholars of Canada ; we can in all fairness hope to do something towards ornamenting, at least, the trees and fences of our common inheritance ; and, if our labours be unimportant in the general forthputting of Celtic ardour for Celtic learning, we can console ourselves by believing with Cicero that *prima sequentem pulchrum est in secundis tertiisque consistere.* We can prevent our zeal from growing lukewarm or listless, by applying to ourselves the answer of the brave Spartan at Thermopylæ, when his attention was drawn in a forcible manner to the overwhelming strength of foe : *pugnabimus umbra.* Nor, if fortune attends us, can we be at a loss to determine the particular manner in which we can be of service to Celtic literature. Our Manx cousins tell us, " When comes the day will come its counsel with it : *Tra hig yn laa, hig yn coyrle lesh.*"

We are, as a Society, in our infancy : let us for the moment abandon the lofty indifference which animated many of our ancestors when material interests were at stake. Let us believe that even to Celtic Societies these well-known words apply :

Haud facile emergunt quorum virtutibus obstat
Res angusta domi.

Sidney Smith, when the Edinburgh Review was established, proposed as a motto " Tenui musam meditamur avena," words which he translated with characteristic originality : " *We cultivate literature upon a little oatmeal.*" Our faith, however, is strong even in our oatmeal days as a Society, that our Celtic friends will befriend us liberally ; and, that out of the *material* treasures which their industry and their sagacity have enabled them to accumulate in Canada, they will so aid us that we can procure for ourselves copies of the *literary* treasures of our common race.

We want all the German and French books that deal with Celtic literature and philology. We want, as speedily as possible, copies of all the principal Irish, Scotch, and Welsh MSS. We ought to have the valuable works which perpetuate for the instruction and benefit of the Celts of our own day and of the days that are yet to be, the scholarship, the opinions, and investigations of the ablest, most patriotic and industrious Celts who have ever graced the literary annals of Ireland and Wales, of Scotland and the Isle of Man.

Let us defer to the Ossianic advice, and infuse all the vigour and vitality that we can into our youthful Society.

> "Bithibh treun an tus na teugbhoil;
> 'S e cliu gach neach a cheud iomradh."

We begin our career earnestly and hopefully,—with the determination to honour all our Celtic brethren alike,—to welcome with equal cordialty the aid and sympathy of the Celts of Cape Breton and of Manitoba,—to remember with catholic faithfulness that the same blood warms our veins, and that our only recognition of superior worth will be in proportion to the services which, as Celts of the Dominion of Canada, we can render to the common cause of Celtic literature and Celtic philology,—to the common cause of the noble, and the true, and the useful, and the patriotic among the races of the earth.

Our appeal to the Celts of Canada is in the words of the Irish Epigram :

> "Mas ionmhuinn leat na braithre,
> Bi leo gu sasta socair."

> "An la' chi 's' nach fhaic."

POEM.

By the Bard of the Society.

An am Baile' chnoic rioghail, tha Gaidheil ro-dhileas,
A' deanamh an dichill le eolas nach gann ;
A cantuinn, 's a' leughadh, 's a' sgriobhadh na canain
A labhradh an Eden : 's i' Ghaelig a bh' ann.

A luchd teagaisg na Beurla, bithibh tosdach le cheile,
Tha commun ag eiridh 's an t-saoghal so mu thuath ;
Comunn Oiseineach aluinn a' teagasg na Gaelig :
'S iad fior chlann nan Gaidheal a chumas i suas.

Nach seall sibh mu'n cuairt air ard—sgoilearan uasal,
'S a' Ghaelig 'n a buannachd a thuigsinn gach cainnt ;
A dh' ionnsachadh Greugais, Eabhra, Laidin, 'us Beurla,
A chionn gur i freumh do gach canain a th' ann.

Biodh an t—aineolach taireil, mar is minic a bha e,
Theid a' chainnt a bha' m Parras a chumail an aird ;
Anns an duthaich a dh' fhag sinn, tha moran d'ar braithrean
A' seinn anns a' Ghaelig cliu Oisein, am bard.

Biodh an comunn so dileas 'us laidir 'us lionmhor ;
'S bithidh moran r'a innseadh le firinn 's r'a luadh,
Mu na beachdan a sgaoil sinn, a' lionadh an t-saoghail so,
Le Gaelig ro-fheumail 's le eolas 'bhios buan.

Agus cluinnidh na h-altain a thig ann ar deigh-ne,
Mar sgriobh 'us mar leugh sinn a' chanain a's fearr :
'Us 'nuair chuireas sinn crioch air gach dleasdanas a ni sinn,
Innsidh eachdruidh fhirinneach c'uin, agus c'ait.

Le ciad mile failt do gach aon a tha lathair,
A chum onoir na Gaelig a mhaireas gach re,
Biodh Baile' chnoic rioghail 'n a bheannachd do mhiltean,
Agus canain nan Gaidheal cho maireann riu fein.

THE CELTIC SOCIETY, MONTREAL.

(Translation of the foregoing.)

In the Royal Mountain City there are noble men to-day,
Speaking, reading, writing Gaelic in the good old Highland way ;
Men of talent, men of learning, and their language they uphold ;
Who will say 'twas not in Eden it was spoken first of old ?

Ye who speak and teach the English, knowing nothing more at all,
Cease your scorning and derision, for at famous Montreal
Met in union purely Celtic, there are men of mightier powers,
And the star of learning brightens in this northern world of ours.

Look around among the mighty, where the brightest scholars are,
See how they, or else their fathers, came from Scotia's hills afar ;
Where in language most expressive, living bards delight to tell
Of the days when gifted Ossian touched the Celtic lyre so well.

Let this Ossianic Union, or Association, grow,
Till the world is well instructed in the truth that all should know ;
That however long neglected, the old Celtic is the best,
Most expressive language spoken, and the root of all the rest.

How it helps the Hebrew scholar, and the man who studies Greek,
Fills philologists with wonder, teaches how to write and speak ;
Hence how wise to stand united as a true and noble band
To perpetuate the Gaelic in our own, our favoured land?

While we share the fruits arising from extending Gaelic lore,
We shall leave a boon to others, when our mission work is o'er ;
Yes, a priceless store of knowledge, if we do our duty now ;
And the scroll of Time shall publish, where we did it, when, and how.

Then " a hundred thousand welcomes " to the friends who join with us
To explain, maintain, and cherish the pure Celtic language thus ;
So the Royal Mountain city shall our Canada adorn,
With its colleges a blessing to the millions yet unborn.

APPENDIX.

This Society was organized on the 6th of December, 1883. And the Bard of the Society, Mr. Arch. McKillop, recited in Gaelic and English a poem composed by him in honour of the occasion, and also recited another Gaelic poem composed by himself.

The first regular meeting was held on the 25th of January, 1884, at which the President, Rev. Dr. McNish, delivered his Inaugural Address, followed with the recitation of an original Gaelic poem by the Bard of the Society.

The following is a list of the papers received and read at the Society's meetings, ending 30th April, 1885, viz :—

WM. GREIG, Sr., Montreal.—" The British, who are they and what are they ?"—Read 28th February, 1884.

J. K. WARD, Montreal.—" Geographical and Historical Account of the Isle of Man."—Read 28th February, 1884.

D. B. BLAIR, Nova Scotia.—" Rudiments of Gaelic Grammar."—Read March 27th, 1884.

NEIL McNEIL BRODIE, Halifax, N.S.—" Influence of Eisteddfods on the Welsh Language."—Read October 30th, 1884.

DR. McNISH, Cornwall.—" Celtic Prosody."—Read 5th February, 1885.

REV. D. B. BLAIR, Barney's River, N.S.—"The Early Settlement of the Lower Provinces by the Scottish Gael, their various situations and present condition."—Read 5th February, 1885.

GEO. SANDFIELD McDONALD, B.A., Cornwall, Ont. — "The Literary Aspect of the Keltic Settlements in the Counties of Stormont and Glengarry."—Read 5th February, 1885.

HUGH McCOLL, Strathroy, Ont.—"Sketches of Highland Settlements in Western Ontario, and Literary Productions of Highlanders there." —Read 26th February, 1885.

D. W. ROWLAND, St. Thomas, Ont.—"The Madoc, or Welsh Indians."— Read 26th February, 1885.

Rev. Robt. Campbell, M.A., Montreal.—"The Influence of St. Columba on Celtic Literature."—Read 12th March, 1885.

J. K. Ward, Montreal.—"Historical Sketch of the Isle of Man."

Neil McNeil Brodie, Halifax, N.S.—"Similarity between the Irish and the Scotch Gaelic."—Read 26th March, 1885.

Wm. Greig, Sr., Montreal.—"Who are we?"—Read 26th March, 1885.

Rev. John McKay, Strathclair, Manitoba.—Extracts from a paper on the "Celts in the North West."—Read by Rev. Dr. McNish, 30th April, 1885.

Dr. McNish, Cornwall.—"The Cornish Language."—Read 30th April, 1885.

Besides the foregoing, several original poems, the work of the Society's Bard, were recited by him.

The following contributions to the Society's Library have been thankfully received :—

"Language and Literature of the Scottish Highlands," presented by the Author, Prof. Blackie, of Edinburgh.

"A Manx Dictionary," by J. K. Ward, Esq.

"Matt. Arnold, On the Study of Celtic Literature," and "Evan McColl's Poems and Songs," by Wm. Drysdale, Esq.

"The Gaelic Kingdom in Scotland," presented by the Author, Mr. Chas. Stewart, Tigh an Duin, of Killin, Scotland.

"Modern Specimens of Gaelic, Welsh and Manx Literature," presented by Neil McNeil Brodie, Esq , Halifax, N.S.

"Dr. Kelly's Manx Grammar," presented by Dr. McNish.

"Manx Antiquities," presented by J. K. Ward.

"Clarsach Na Coille," presented by Jas. McLennan, Q.C., Toronto.

"The Book of Common Prayer" in Manx, presented by Rev. W. Kermode, Isle of Man.

"The Manx Note Book," (two numbers to date), presented by the Editor, A. H, Moore, Isle of Man.

Two Pamphlets from Dr. Ernest Windisch, Leipsig.

Several Pamphlets from M. Eug. Beauvois, France.

The following six volumes were presented to the Society by the Author, A. McKenzie, Esq., F.S.A., Editor of the " Celtic Magazine" :—
" The Isle of Skye," " The History of the Highland Clearances," " Analysis of the Crofter Royal Commission," " History of the Camerons," " The History and Genealogy of the MacDonalds of Glengarry," "The History and Genealogy of the Macdonalds of Glenranald," also " The Life of Flora MacDonald," by Rev. A. MacGregor, M.A., and " Sketches of the Highlanders," by General D. Stewart, of Garth.

LIST OF MEMBERS.

Life Members.

D. McTaggart,	Montreal.
J. K. Ward,	"
John MacLennan,	Lancaster, Ontario.
Duncan Monroe,	Cornwall, "
Roderick R. McLennan,	Cornwall, "
Patk. Purcell,	Summerston, "
Alexander G. Watson,	Cornwall "

Members.

Rev. N. MacNish. B.D., LL.D., - - - - - - Cornwall.

Rev. Principal MacVicar, D.D., LL.D., Member of the "Société d'Ethnographie," and "Athénée Orientale." - Montreal.

Rev. Professor Campbell, M.A., M.S.R. Rouman; Del. Gen. et Med. Institution Ethnographique, etc., etc. - - - Montreal.

Rev. Professor Coussirat, B.D., B.A., Officier d'Academie, "

Rev. W. J. Dey, M.A., - - - - - - - - "

Rev. Robert Campbell, M.A., - - - - - - "

Donald McLean, - - Student Presbyterian College, "

John C. Martin, - - - - " " "

Malcolm J. McLeod, - - - " " "

Murdoch McKenzie, - - - " " "

J. W. McKenzie, B.A., - - - " " "

Colin McKerchar, - - - - " " "

Rev. Malcolm L. Leitch, - - - " " Valleyfield.

John Lewis, - - - - - - - - Montreal.

J. B. McLea, - - - - - - - - - "

Donald McKenzie, - - - - - - - - "

Wm. Greig, Sr., - - - - - - - - - "

Wm. Greig, Jr., - - - - - - - - - "

Edward Armour, - - - - - - - - - "

Wm. Drysdale, - - - - - - - - - "

A. McLennan, - - - - - - - - Montreal.
Jas. Stewart, M.D., - - - - Professor McGill College, "
Hector Buie, - - - - - - - - - "
Allan Livingston, - - - - - - - - "
Alex. D. Lanskail, - - - - - - - "
Arch. McKillop (Bard)
Wm. C. Davidson, - - - - - - - - Montreal.
J. M. Kirk, - - - - - - - - - - "
Rev. J. Matheson, - - - - - - - Martintown.
Donald C. Munro, - - - - - - - - "
James McArthur, - - - - - - - - "
Rev. A. McGillivray, - - - - - - Williamstown.
D. McLennan, - - - - - - - "
Rev. Geo. Coull, M.A., - - - - - - Valleyfield, Q.
Donald K. MacKinnon, - - - - - South Finch, Ont.
Miss Victoria S. Campbell, - - - - Montreal.
Henry Kavanagh, - - - - - - - "
Thos. Kneen, - - - - - - - - "
Thos. Loomis, - - - - - - - Buffalo, U.S.
Dr. Bergin, M.P., Surgeon General, - - - Cornwall, Ont.
Duncan A. McDonald, - - - - - " "
George McDonnell, - - - - - - " "
Wm. Chisholm, - - - - - - - " "
Alex. F. McDonald, - - - - - - " "
Peter Ernest Campbell, - - - - - " "
Dugald McPherson, - - - - - Glanworth, "
John McKerchar, LL.B., - - - - - Montreal.
Geo. Sandfield McDonald, B.A., - - - - Cornwall, Ont.
Henry Corran, - - - - - - - Montreal.
James Ogle, - - - - - - Cornwall Centre, Ont.
Alex. McCracken, - - - - - - Cornwall, "
T. W. Harrington, - - - - - - - Montreal.
John Purcell, - - - - - - - Cornwall.
M. C. Mullarky, - - - - - - - Montreal.
Patk. Gildea Mulhern, - - - - - - Cornwall.
Angus McIntyre, - - - - - - - "
Jas. Wright, - - - - - - - - Montreal.

Honorary Members.

Rt.-Hon. Sir J. A. Macdonald, P.C., K.C.B.,	Ottawa.
Hon. D. A. Macdonald,	Montreal.
Sir D. L. MacPherson,	Toronto.
Hon. A. Mackenzie,	"
Hon. G. W. Ross, LL.B.,	"
E. B. Greenshields,	Montreal.
K. Campbell,	"
A. Campbell,	"
Sheriff MacIntyre,	Cornwall.
D. B. MacLennan, Q.C.,	"
Sheriff MacKellar,	Hamilton.
Donald Cameron,	Windsor.
Alex. MacPherson,	Montreal.
Evan McColl,	Kingston.
Rev. D. Masson, M.D., M.A.,	Edinburgh, Scotland.
Rev. Dr. MacLauchlan,	" "
Rev. A. Clerk, LL.D.,	Kilmallie, "
Rev. A. Sinclair,	Kenmore, "
Rev. J. McKerchar,	Avoch, "
James McKerchar, Banker,	Aberfeldy, "
Sheriff Nicholson, LL.D.,	Kirkcudbright, "
Rev. J. McKay, D.D.,	Inverness, "
David Morrice, Esq.,	Montreal.
Hon. D. A. Smith,	"
Colonel Walker,	"
Alex. Milloy,	"
Hon. Justice Proudfoot,	Toronto.
Rev. Wm. Reeves, D.D.,	Armagh, Ireland.
Hon. T. B. MacInnes, M.D.,	New Westminster, British Columbia.
Hon. Donald McMillan,	Alexandria, Ont.
Lachlan MacCallum,	Stromness, "

44

Corresponding Members.

PROF. J. S. BLACKIE, - - - - - - Edinburgh, Scotland.
WM. F. SKENE, Esq., D.C.L., LL.D., Historiographer Royal," "
PROF. DONALD MACKINNON, M.A., - - - " "
MRS. MARY MACKELLAR, - - - - - " "
NEIL MACLEOD, Esq., - - - - - - " "
ALEX. MACKENZIE, (Celt Mag.) - - - - Inverness, "
REV. J. MACTAVISH, - - - - - - " "
PROF. JOYCE, LL.D., - - - - - - Dublin, Ireland.
PROF. BRIEN O'LOONEY, M.R.I.A., &c., - - - " "
PROF. RHYS, M.A., - - - - - - - Oxford, England.
DR. EDWARDS, - - - - - - - - North Wales.
M. EUGENE BEAUVOIS, - - - - - Corberon, Côte d'Or, France.
JOHN FRASER, Esq., M.A., - - - - Maitland, N.S.W.
REV. PROF. NICHOLSON, M.A., - - - - - Kingston.
PROF. HARRIS, C.E., - - - - - - - "
REV. DR. MACLEOD, - - - - - - Sidney, C.B.
HUGH LAMONT, - - - - - - - - P.E.I.
COLIN MACPHEE, - - - - - - - "
NEIL MACNEILL BRODIE, - - - - Halifax, N.S.
HON. A. B. MACKENZIE, - - - Charlottetown, P.E.I.
NEIL MCGILLIVRAY, - - - Inverness, Scotland.
D. SPENCE, - - - - - - - - Toronto.
D. MCEWEN, - - - - - - - Cornwall.
REV. WM. R. SUTHERLAND, - - - Strathburn, Ont.
REV. DR. LAMONT, - - - - - Marsboro, Que.
REV. JOHN FERGUSON, - - - - Vankleek Hill.
REV. D. H. FLETCHER, - - - - - Hamilton.
REV. D. GORDON, - - - - - - Harrington.
REV. J. FRASER, - - - - - - St. Elmo.
REV. F. MACLENNAN, - - - - - Dunvegan.
REV. N. MCKINNON, - - - - - Kilmartin.
REV. J. MILLOY, - - - - - - Crinan.
REV. JOHN MCKAY, - - - - - Strathclair, Manitoba.
REV. JOHN MORRISON, - - - - - Cedarville.
REV. J. L. MURRAY, M.A., - - - - - Kincardine.

Rev. D. B. Cameron, - - - - - - - Acton, Ontario.
Hugh MacColl, - - - - - - - - Strathroy, "
Rev. A. F. MacQueen, - - - - - - Ripley, "
Charles Stewart, Esq., Tigh an Duin, - - - Killin, Scotland.
Hugh McLean, Esq., - - Brecklarach Tarbert, Argyleshire, "
Rev. A. McLean Sinclair, - - - - - - Springville, N.S.
Rev. D. B. Blair, - - - - - - Barney's River, N.S.
Michael McDonald, - - - - Grand Lake, near Sydney, C.B.
Hugh Fraser, - - - - - - - - Embro, Ont.
Wm. Spurrell, - - - - - - Caermarthen, South Wales.
John Fleming, - - - - - - - - Dublin, Ireland.
Henry Whyte, - - - - - - - - Oban, Scotland.
Rev. Mr. Cameron, - - - - - Brodick, Arran, "
Rev. Mr. Ross, - - - - - - - Glasgow, "
Rev. Donald MacCallum, - - - - Waternish, Skye, "
Rev. Alex. Stewart, LL.D., - - - - Fort William, "
John Campbell, - - - - - Ledaig, near Oban, "
Rev. Dr. Thomas, - - - - - - - - Toronto, Ont.
Rev. D. W. Rowland, - - - - - - St. Thomas, "
Duncan MacGregor Crerar, - - - - - New York.
Chas. Garrison, - - - Montauban, Tarn-et-Garonne, France.
C. T. C. Callow, Advocate, - - - - - Douglas, Isle of Man.
Rev. W. Kermode, M.A., - - - - - Ballaugh, " "
A. W. Moore, M.A., - - - - - Cronkbourne, " "
Rev. Wm. Drury, - - - - - Kirk Braddon, " "
Rev. Donald Fraser, M.A., - - - - - - Victoria, B.C.
James McLennan, Q.C., - - - - - - Toronto, Ont.
Henri Gaidoz, Editeur *Revue Celtique*, - - - - - - Paris.
Dr. Ernest Windisch, - - - - - - Leipsig University.
Robt. Greig, F.E.I.S., - - - - Munlochy, Rossshire, Scotland.
John Greig, - - - - - - - Sunderland, England.

·